D0397074

Copyright © 1992
Peter Pauper Press, Inc.
202 Mamaroneck Avenue
White Plains, NY 10601
All rights reserved
ISBN 0-88088-756-7
Printed in Hong Kong
7 6 5 4 3 2 1

INSPIRATION
FOR LIVING

If you think you can do a thing or think you can't do a thing, you're right.

Henry Ford

No one can make you feel inferior without your consent.

Eleanor Roosevelt

Every life is a play in which
the lead character is center
stage—and the lead character
in your life is *you*.

Sonya Friedman

When I tune in to my
beautiful self, I get happiness.
Everything in the universe
belongs to me.

Dick Gregory

If rejection destroys your self-esteem, you're letting others hold you as an emotional hostage.

Brian Tracy

Poor is the man whose pleasures depend on the permission of another.

Madonna

I have an everyday religion
that works for me: Love
yourself first and everything
else falls into line.

Lucille Ball

You gain strength, courage
and confidence by every
experience in which you
really stop to look fear in the
face.

Eleanor Roosevelt

Self-love seems so often
unrequited.

Anthony Powell

I've got more confidence
than I do talent, I think. I
think confidence is the main
achiever of success.

Dolly Parton

It's not what you are that holds you back, it's what you think you are not.

Denis Waitley

I think one must finally take one's life in one's arms.

Arthur Miller,
After the Fall

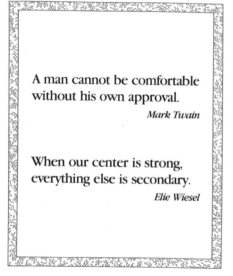

A man cannot be comfortable
without his own approval.

Mark Twain

When our center is strong,
everything else is secondary.

Elie Wiesel

He who walks in another's tracks leaves no footprints.

Joan Brannon

Self-confidence is not in finding the first step but in feeling sure that a first step can be found.

Robert Mende

Life only demands from you
the strength you possess.
Only one feat is possible—
not to have run away.

Dag Hammarskjold

There *is* a fountain of youth:
It is your mind, your talents,
the creativity you bring in
your life and the lives of
people you love.

Sophia Loren

If I am not for myself, who
will be for me? And if I am
only for myself, what am I?
And if not now—when?

Hillel

To love oneself is the
beginning of a life-long
romance.

Oscar Wilde

The mind is its own place,
and in itself, can make heaven
of Hell, a hell of Heaven.

John Milton

You must do the thing you
think you cannot do.

Eleanor Roosevelt

If you don't run your own life, somebody else will.

John Atkinson

Lack of confidence is not the result of difficulty; the difficulty comes from lack of confidence.

Seneca

Yes, you can be a dreamer
and a doer too, if you will
remove one word from your
vocabulary: *Impossible*.

Robert H. Schuller

To the possession of the self
the way is inward.

Plotinus

This above all: to thine own
   self be true,
And it must follow, as the
   night the day, Thou canst
not then be false
   to any man.

Shakespeare,
Hamlet

Man is what he believes.

Anton Chekhov

If one advances confidently,
in the direction of his own
dreams and endeavors, to
lead the life which he has
imagined, he will meet with a
success unexpected in
common hours.

Thoreau

Love is the miracle cure.
Loving ourselves works
miracles in our lives.

Louise Hay

In order to become the winner that you will respect and admire . . . you must have control of the authorship of your own destiny . . . the pen that writes your life story *must* be held in your own hand.

Irene C. Kassorla

Without self-confidence we are as babes in the cradle.

Virginia Woolf

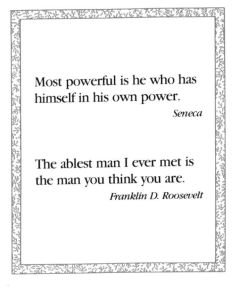

Most powerful is he who has
himself in his own power.

Seneca

The ablest man I ever met is
the man you think you are.

Franklin D. Roosevelt

What seems different in yourself—that's the rare thing you possess. The one thing that gives each of us his worth, and that's just what we try to suppress. And we claim to love life.

André Gide

A man is the sum of his actions, of what he has *done*, of what he can do. Nothing else.

André Malraux

Remember: *you are the only person who thinks in your mind!* You are the power and authority in your world.

Louise Hay

The direction of change to seek is not in our four dimensions: it is getting deeper into what you are, where you are, like turning up the volume on the amplifier.

Thaddeus Golas

Make a true estimate of your own ability, then raise it 10 per cent.

Norman Vincent Peale

The best years of your life are the ones in which you decide your problems are your own. You don't blame them on your mother, the ecology or the President. You realize that you control your own destiny.

Albert Ellis

No man remains quite what
he was when he recognizes
himself.

Thomas Mann

Before all else, each of us
must take a fundamental
risk—to be true to ourselves.

Jim Webb

There is overwhelming evidence that the higher the level of self-esteem, the more likely one will treat others with respect, kindness, and generosity. People who do not experience self-love have little or no capacity to love others.

Nathaniel Branden

The certainty that nothing
can happen to us that does
not in our innermost being
belong to us is the foundation
of fearlessness.

Govinda

Self-confidence is the first
requisite to great undertakings.

Samuel Johnson

It is the chiefest point of happiness that a man is willing to be what he is.

Erasmus

Be gentle with yourself, learn to love yourself, to forgive yourself, for only as we have the right attitude toward ourselves can we have the right attitude toward others.

Wilfred Peterson

Self-trust is the essence of
heroism.

Emerson

Life is just a mirror, and what
you see out there, you must
first see inside of you.

Wally "Famous" Amos

I am my world.

Ludwig Wittgenstein

Trust thyself: every heart
vibrates to that iron string.

Emerson

The man who has confidence
in himself gains the confidence
of others.

Hasidic saying

Depend not on another, but
lean instead on thyself. . . .
True happiness is born of self
reliance.

The laws of Manu

No man should part with his own individuality and become that of another.

Channing

As he thinketh in his heart, so is he.

Book of Proverbs

The possibility of encountering one's reality—learning about one's self—can be frightening and frustrating. Many people expect to discover the *worst*. A hidden fear lies in the fact that they may also discover the *best*.

Muriel James and
Dorothy Jongeward

The duty to be alive is the same as the duty to become oneself, to develop into the individual one potentially is.

Erich Fromm

You have no idea what a poor opinion I have of myself—and how little I deserve it.

W. S. Gilbert

When you are no longer
compelled by desire or
fear . . . when you have seen
the radiance of eternity in all
the forms of time . . . when
you follow your bliss . . .
doors will open where you
would not have thought
there were doors . . . and the
world will step in and help.

Joseph Campbell

It came to me that having life itself, life being such a miraculous achievement, is like winning the grand prize. What we do after that—what we do with our lives—is the frosting on the cake.

Earl Nightingale

There's only one corner of the universe you can be certain of improving, and that's your own self.

Aldous Huxley

How can you come to know yourself? Never by thinking; always by doing. Try to do your duty, and you'll know right away what you amount to. And what is your duty? Whatever the day calls for.

Goethe

The more self-knowledge you acquire, the less you will have to wonder about yourself.

Wayne Dyer

He that respects himself is
    safe from others;
He wears a coat of mail that
    none can pierce.

Longfellow

Doubt whom you will, but
never doubt yourself.

Christian Nestell Bovee

Somehow I can't believe that there are any heights that can't be scaled by a man who knows the secret of making his dreams come true. This special secret, it seems to me, can be summarized in four C's. They are Curiosity, Confidence, Courage and Constancy and the greatest of these is confidence. When you believe in a thing, believe in it all the way.

Walt Disney

You are your thoughts. Don't ever let anyone else have dominion over them.

Shad Helmstetter

Our imagination is the only limit to what we can hope to have in the future.

Charles F. Kettering

Self-love is the instrument of our preservation; it resembles the provision for the perpetuity of mankind—it is necessary, it is dear to us, it gives us pleasure, and we must possess it.

Voltaire

They can conquer who believe they can.

Virgil

It is hard to fight an enemy who has outposts in your head.

Sally Kempton

A man can stand a lot as long as he can stand himself.

Axel Munthe

Just trust yourself, then you will know how to live.

Goethe

No matter who or what made you what you have become, that doesn't release you from the responsibility of making yourself over into what you ought to be.

Ashley Montagu

Being authentic, being actually and precisely what you claim to be . . . requires that your behavior prove your claim.

John Hanley

I don't know the key to success, but the key to failure is trying to please everybody.

Bill Cosby

We come to feel as we
behave.

Paul Pearsall

Self-respect is the noblest
garment with which a man
may clothe himself, the most
elevating feeling with which
the mind can be inspired.

Samuel Smiles

Our lives improve only when we take chances—and the first and most difficult risk we can take is to be honest with ourselves.

Walter Anderson

You have the greatest chance of being happy when the voice you respond to is your *own* voice.

Sonya Friedman

Respect gods before demi-
gods, heroes before men, and
first among men your parents;
but respect yourself most
of all.

Pythagoras

There are admirable potenti-
alities in every human being.
Believe in your strength and
your youth. Learn to repeat
endlessly to yourself: "It all
depends on me."

André Gide

Self-respect is the corner-
stone of all virtue.

John Herschel

Never, "for the sake of peace
and quiet," deny your own
experience or convictions.

Dag Hammarskjold

Self-respect cannot be hunted. It cannot be purchased. It is never for sale. It cannot be fabricated out of public relations. It comes to us when we are alone, in quiet moments, in quiet places, when we suddenly realize that, knowing the good, we have done it; knowing the beautiful, we have served it; knowing the truth, we have spoken it.

Whitney Griswold

Development of character
consists solely in moving
toward self-sufficiency.

Quentin Crisp

Self-approbation, when found
in truth and a good con-
science, is a source of some
of the purest joys known to
man.

Charles Simmons

Just be what you are and speak from your guts and heart—it's all a man has.

Hubert H. Humphrey

You are everything that is, your thoughts, your life, your dreams come true. You are everything you choose to be. You are as unlimited as the endless universe.

Shad Helmstetter

Self-reliance is the only road
to true freedom, and being
one's own person is its
ultimate reward.

Patricia Sampson

How many cares one loses
when one decides not to be
something but to be someone.

Coco Chanel

Self-esteem is the reputation
we acquire with ourselves.

Nathaniel Branden

Power is strength and the
ability to see yourself through
your own eyes and not
through the eyes of another.
It is being able to place a
circle of power at your own
feet . . .

Agnes Whistling Elk

The questions which one asks oneself begin, at last, to illuminate the world, and become one's key to the experience of others. One can only face in others what one can face in oneself. On this confrontation depends the measure of our wisdom and compassion.

James Baldwin

Go to your bosom;
Knock there; and ask your
heart, what it doth know.

Shakespeare,
Measure for Measure

If you do not believe in
yourself, do not blame others
for lacking faith in you.

Brendan Francis

Look well into thyself; there
is a source of strength which
will always spring up if thou
wilt always look there.

Marcus Aurelius

Risk! Risk anything! Care no
more for the opinions of
others, for those voices. Do
the hardest thing on earth for
you. Act for yourself.

Katherine Mansfield

Like one who lives in a valley and then crosses the mountains and sees the plain, he knows now from experience that the sign saying "Do not go beyond this point," like the high mountains, does not signify a barrier.

Alice Miller

Love not what you are but only what you may become.

Cervantes

You have to whistle your own tune. You have to walk along the track yourself. Nobody else can lead you. Nobody else can really help you. Once you get the feeling that it is your responsibility, it is the most freeing thing in the world.

Pat Carroll

Only I can change my life. No one can do it for me.

Carol Burnett

Happiness is having a sense of self—not a feeling of being perfect but of being good enough and knowing that you are in the process of growth, of being, of achieving levels of joy.

Leo F. Buscaglia

If you do not know your own identity, who is going to identify you?

Thomas Merton

No one will ever breathe one breath for us. No one will ever think one thought that is ours. No one will *ever* stand in our bodies, experience what happens to us, feel our fears, dream our dreams, or cry our tears. . . . No one else can ever live a single moment of our lives for us. That we must do for ourselves.

Shad Helmstetter

Man often becomes what he believes himself to be. If I keep on saying to myself that I cannot do a certain thing, it is possible that I may end by really becoming incapable of doing it. On the contrary, if I have the belief that I can do it, I shall surely acquire the capacity to do it even if I may not have it at the beginning.

Mahatma Gandhi

A strong positive mental attitude will create more miracles than any wonder drug.

Patricia Neal

What lies behind us and what lies before us are tiny matters compared to what lies within us.

Emerson

In each of us are places
where we have never gone.
. . . Only by pressing the
limits do you ever find them.

Dr. Joyce Brothers

There is no dependence that
can be sure but a dependence
upon one's self.

John Gay

As for worrying about what other people might think— forget it. They aren't concerned about you. They're too busy worrying about what you and other people think of them.

Michael LeBoeuf

A wise man never loses anything if he have himself.

Montaigne

Everyone should carefully observe which way his heart draws him, and then choose that way with all his strength.

Hasidic saying

Self-reliance is the answer to the question, "Who can I turn to?"

Patricia Sampson

Courage means flying in the face of criticism, relying on yourself, being willing to accept and learn from the consequences of all your choices. It means believing enough in yourself and in living your life as you choose so that you cut the strings whose ends other people hold and use to pull you in contrary directions.

Wayne Dyer

When we know that the *cause* of something is in ourselves, and that we (ourselves) are one of the few things in this universe that we have the right and the ability to change, we begin to get a sense of the choices we really do have, an inkling of the power we have, a feeling of being in charge— of our lives, of our future, of our dreams.

John-Roger and
Peter McWilliams

You are your most important critic. There is no opinion so vitally important to your well-being as the opinion you have of yourself. And the most important meetings, briefings, and conversations you'll ever have are the conversations you will have with yourself.

Denis Waitley

Be confident. Be expectant of grand and beautiful results from everything you do.

Patricia Sampson

Every single man is a new thing in the world and is called upon to fulfill his particularity in this world.

Martin Buber

Happiness is intrinsic, it's an internal thing. When you build it into yourself, no external circumstances can take it away. That kind of happiness is a twenty-four-hour thing.

Leo F. Buscaglia

The way you treat yourself sets the standard for others.

Sonya Friedman

Let every man's hope be in himself.

Virgil

Risk-taking is not easy—and the greatest risk of all is to try to know oneself, and to act on that knowledge.

Walter Anderson